Using
Your
Emotions
Creatively

Using Your Emotions Creatively

Garnett M. Wilder

God intends us to have lives of joyful fulfillment

Previously printed 1984 Judson Press, Valley Forge, PA

The Scripture quotations in this publication are from the Revised Standard Version of the Bible copyrighted 1946, 1952 © 1971, 1973 by the Division of Christian Education of the National Council of the Churches of Christ in the U.S.A., and used by permission.

ISBN: 1-890307-22-X

Published by
Boyd Publishing Company
Milledgeville, GA 31061
1999

About the Author

GARNETT MARION WILDER was born in Carrollton, Georgia, on March 22, 1930. He made his commitment to Christ at the age of nine years under the preaching of evangelist, Harry Denman. He was called to preach at the age of 14 years.

Dr. Wilder received the B.A. degree with a major in history from the University of Georgia in 1951. He received the Bachelor of Divinity degree *cum laude* in 1954 from the Candler School of Theology of Emory University. He studied in the Ph.D. program of Drew University, Madison, New Jersey. While at Drew, he assisted in the translation for publication of Friedrich Gogarten's book, The Reality of Faith. Dr. Wilder studied in the Graduate School of Emory University from which he received the Ph.D. degree in Systematic Theology in August, 1959.

Dr. Wilder taught theology for 20 years in the Course of Study School, Candler School of Theology, Emory University.

Dr. Wilder served with distinction as a United Methodist minister in North Georgia for 48 years.

Dr. Wilder is the author of three published books: Promises to Keep, Between the Times, and Using Your Emotions Creatively.

Dr. Wilder was married to the former Marian Pinson of Athens, Georgia. The Wilders have three children and nine grandchildren. The Wilders lived in Avondale Estates, Georgia, until his death in November, 1998. Dr. Wilder died in the pulpit of the Decatur First United Methodist Church as he concluded preaching.

Dr. Wilder will be remembered as a faithful servant of God whose integrity, courage and intellect made a bold witness for Christ. He was a true prophet!

The second edition of this book was printed at the request of his many friends and former students.

Contents

Using Your Emotions Creatively

Introduction

We have lived through the "age of reason," and now we come to the "age of rhetoric." More words are being catapulted onto the scene of human affairs than ever before. We contend with an onslaught of words not only from family, friends, and neighbors but also from all over the world. The word explosion in our time is accompanied by a release of emotion that is threatening to overwhelm our society. Emotions have become rampant. We no longer hold so tenaciously to the fanciful notion that we are civilized. From every direction comes the solemn reminder: our emotions are not to be trusted in a complex, highly frustrating environment. We must give attention to the stormy impulses within us that from time to time express themselves in such alarming ways.

Self-control has been a tantalizing ideal for persons since the earliest recorded history. For the most part, it has remained merely an ideal, an unrealized dream. Whenever we have thought that civilization was making progress toward the kind of self-mastery that might allow persons to live together in peace, another storm of emotion and conflict would brew into being, and some segment of society would explode into chaos (usually war). Every time a person or nation erupts emotionally, we are graphically reminded of the stormy impulses that stir within us.

It is quite significant to me that modern psychology, with all its effort to be scientifically precise, agrees so wholeheartedly with the Bible while the Bible has made little or no conscious effort to be scientifically precise. For example, the first three chapters of the book of Genesis present man and woman in conflict within themselves. The conflict is between their impulses to satisfy their own desires and the claim of responsibility upon them. Humankind is seen in rebellion against the claim of a higher reality. The founder of psychoanalysis, Sigmund Freud, observed that the fundamental motivational impulse of humans is to satisfy their instinctual urges. Frustrations, repressions, and psychodestructive guilts result when these urges run afoul of the superego or conscience. Later developments in psychology have not refuted this basic observation of the struggle between desire and conscience.

There is no doubt that we must deal with the problem of our emotions. We must learn to control them. There are those who conclude that control is neither necessary nor advisable. They say that it is the effort to control emotions that results in social and individual outbursts. This kind of thinking goes back at least as far as the Greeks of the first century before Christ. Some of them said, "Let a man express himself." Although self-control was regarded as a virtue by the Greeks and Romans, they also worshipped the instinctual part of themselves. *Dionysus* was god of appetite and fertility. *Mars* was god of war and *Venus* was goddess of love and beauty.

In our own time Nazi Germany developed an entire cultural thrust around the idea of the manifest destiny of the strong over the weak. Self-assertion became the new morality. Adolf Hitler's thought was informed to a significant degree by the philosophy of Friedrich Nietzsche who regarded Christianity as the great perverter of human instinct. Subsequent developments in Nazi Germany demonstrated that absolute self-expression produces inhuman behavior. The Nazis developed the extermination ovens of Auschwitz and Buchenwald and created maternity camps for genetic experimentation. These camps remain a sordid reminder of what can happen to the finest of human civilizations when it allows the instincts of persons to dominate their higher values. No, absolute free expression of human impulses is not a viable alternative to self-control.

A second alternative is equally unacceptable and that is to brand all human instincts as evil instincts to be destroyed rather than controlled. This is what Buddhism seeks to achieve: the eradication of desire. Gautama Buddha believed that suffering is caused by desire. If a person would find peace of soul, he or she must first eliminate desire.

It is true that Buddha's Eightfold Path is a noble way to achieve morality. Nevertheless, there is a sense in which it violates the creative activity of God. Human creativity is tied to emotional urges. One destroys the creative thrust of personality by cutting desire at the roots. This is throwing out the baby with the bath water. The goal is not to reach a state of nothingness. The goal of human life is to achieve responsibly.

J. Wallace Hamilton, a former pastor of the United Methodist Church in St. Petersburg, Florida, said, "Any religion which has as its goal the reduction of desire has no kinship with Christianity." St. Augustine has given us a clue to an answer in his *Confessions:* "Thou has created us for thyself, and our hearts are restless until they find their rest in thee." Persons were made for something more than the unrestricted expression of their instinctual urges. But instinctual urges *were* created for something. They were made to be used in responsible creativity.

A recent development in psychology sheds light on this insight. On the one hand we have heretofore regarded our instincts as inherently good and as urges to be expressed at will. On the other hand, we have viewed desire as evil, something to be destroyed. Psychologists are now emphasizing what the church has been teaching for two thousand years, the importance of the will. The Viennese psychiatrist Viktor Frankl says that the instincts only make proposals. They only suggest, while the will decides what to do with these suggestions. Frankl uses the analogy of a ship. He says, "Sailing does not consist in letting a boat be driven by the wind; rather the art of the sailor is his ability to use the wind in order to be driven in a given direction so that he is able to sail even against the wind."[1]

The biblical answer is that we are to submit our wills to the will of God. We are to use the emotions that we have in responding to God's direction. Fear, anger, and disappointment need not be destructive. They may be "spur[s] at the flank of life," driving us in the direction God would have us go. Emotions can be indicators of satisfaction and fulfillment. We can use desire, fear, and anger to increase the boundaries of joy.

If your past experience suggests that this is a Pollyanna approach and can contribute nothing to your handling of your own problems, I urge you to read further. God has created you for joy, happiness, and personal fulfillment. In order to achieve that purpose, you will have to deal constructively with the emotions you often feel and the problems you most often encounter.

[1] Viktor E. Frankl, *The Doctor and the Soul* (New York: Alfred A. Knopf Inc., 1966), pp. 85-86.

Increasing the Boundaries of Joy

If I understand God's purpose as Jesus demonstrated it and emphasized it, God intends that we have lives of joyful fulfillment. We have an intimation of God's intention when we are not happy, when we are not fulfilled, when we feel "down." We suspect that there ought to be something more to life. Those feelings indicate a longing for something more. That "more" is joy. Webster defines "joy" as "the emotion excited by the expectation or acquisition of good." I believe that definition can be expanded to include "a state of being influenced by the awareness of the dominant power of an ultimate good." This awareness transcends immediate circumstances, whether good or bad, and emphasizes a relationship with the "ultimate good."

This is not mere theory. It can be observed every day in the lives of persons. If we take the time to see it, we may be motivated to seek greater joy for our own lives. In my work as a minister I often meet people whose lives are characterized by a joyful awareness of the love of God.

15

Sometimes I seek them out. In one instance I had moved to another church and soon thereafter I visited a woman named Stella. She was the mother of two dear friends whose lives have been of particular significance to me.

From the very first moment of our meeting, Stella made me feel accepted. She had a warm personal dynamic that made me feel good to be in her presence. I felt understood because she knew about the life of a Methodist preacher. As the wife of a preacher, she had experienced the life of the church in a special way. She understood the ups and the downs, the joys, the fulfillments, and the disappointments. This commonality of experience made me feel included in her world.

A year or two after I met her, Stella entered the hospital for surgery. Something went wrong. Although she had been in the hospital for some time, her death was a shock to me. As I began to prepare my thoughts in order to speak at her funeral, I asked several persons to tell me of those qualities that had made her special to them. One person said, "Well, it was her attitude. It was her joy. She enjoyed who she was, what her life was about."

The thing to keep in mind is that Stella had experienced more than a normal amount of physical pain and physical disability. She had been hospitalized numerous times. She had been in a nursing home for a year. She had returned home and had managed with considerable difficulty to maintain her own apartment.

I knew I was on the right track when speaking at her funeral as I referred to her persistence and her diligence amidst adversity. I recalled that she had been seen propped up in bed with a large bowl in her lap, peeling fruit for ambrosia. As I recounted that incident, her grandchildren broke out in spontaneous laughter. The celebration of her joy was complete! Stella had not intended to be robbed of her joy by the adversities of life. She had entered the surgery room with joy, not because she was happy to go but because she was happy in spite of going.

I believe Stella captured and personified the spirit of the early Christians. They were catapulted onto the scene of human history by a profound experience of exultation. When Mary came out of the garden of Joseph of Arimathea, saying, "I have seen the Lord." (see John 20:18) the world took a different turn. The Christian sense of fulfillment and purpose and joy was simply unconquerable!

I think this unconquerable spirit was what Jesus was trying to convey to us. We can have something fulfilling and happy in our lives that transcends the difficult circumstances we encounter. Joy is not a Pollyanna smoothing of difficulties. To be sure, pain is real, difficulties are tremendous, and problems are sometimes overwhelming. Jesus was keenly aware of that! He knew what pain was. He knew what grief was. He knew what loneliness was. He knew the negative emotions intimately. But he also knew a reality that transcended all negative emotions.

Arthur John Gossip has said that one may trace the journey of Jesus through Galilee by the pathway of joy that he created. I can easily envision blind Bartimaeus (Mark 10:46), who had shuffled his way into and around obstacles all his life, jumping and skipping his way through the marketplace of Jericho, shouting "I can see! I can see!"

I can imagine the widow at the village of Nain (Luke 7:11) receiving her dead son alive again at the hands of Jesus. She had been more than devastated by his death. The occasion of her son's death was not merely a moment of agonizing grief. It was a moment of social and economic desolation. I do not know what her thoughts were as she followed her son's bier through the streets of Nain. But I can sense her exultation as she received him alive again! With our modern scientific mind-set, we may not be able to grasp the power of that account. But I think we know well enough the difference between total despair and overwhelming exultation.

We may be more able to identify with the experience of the leper who came to Jesus and announced, "If you will, you can make me clean" (Mark 1:40). The leper had been an outcast. He had been despised, rejected, alienated. He had come to despise himself. His self-worth was zero. He had heard that someone might be able to help him. The leper followed eagerly the trail of joy that led to Jesus. I believe that by the time he actually found Jesus, he was convinced that Jesus could help him. "Lord, if you will, you can make me clean!" Jesus replied without hesitation or equivocation, "I will; be clean" (see Mark 1:40-41). Jesus reached out and touched him.

I have the feeling that the healing was almost anticlimatic for the leper. The real healing came with the touch. When Jesus touched him, the leper was healed in a way that made the condition of his skin a secondary consideration. Jesus restored his self-worth, his self-respect. He touched him. He included him. Already joy was there!

Many people lose their sense of self-worth by being isolated. They feel pushed out, ignored. They do not feel important. This can easily happen with older people. Jesus' pathway of joy ought to remind us all that we are important. We deserve joy because God wants us to have it. Joy does not have to do with our circumstances. They will be what they are.

The eminent psychiatrist Viktor Frankl suggested that people have creative value, material value, and labor value, and the greatest value of all, attitudinal value. The greatest freedom people have is the freedom to choose what our attitude will be in a given circumstance. No one can take that freedom from us. But if we are going to use that freedom, we shall have to overcome the provincialism of a restricted mentality in which our world closes in, our satisfactions become minimal, and we are separated from one another, from God, and from the world.

To increase the boundaries of joy, we must recover our awareness of who we are as children of God. We must find our roots again in the consciousness of the covenant people of God in the Old Testament. Alexander Miller expressed this consciousness well:

> . . . if we are asked to say summarily why God made the world, [we are forced] to affirm that he made it for fun! There is no purpose in it save the purpose of joy: the joy of the Maker in the world of his making, and the derivative and reciprocal joy of the world in the world itself and in him who made it. It is from here that there stems the characteristic Hebrew attitude to the world of things, which has no faintest touch of world-renouncing spirituality about it. It is rather a lip-smacking, exuberant delight in the ingenious beauty and variety of the created world. . . .[1]

I like that expression, "a lip-smacking, exuberant delight in the ingenious beauty and variety of the created world." We need to recover that delight. If you want to increase the boundaries of your joy, wake up to your world! Push back the walls of your house. Get into the out-of-doors. Enjoy the flowers, the trees, the sunrise, the birds. Enjoy those things that have personal or sentimental value to you. A friend of mine carries a magnifying glass with him so that he can enjoy a range of awareness that most of us miss.

I visit many people who have moved from a house into an apartment. Whether it becomes their home usually depends on their attitude. I have noticed that it seems to help the adjustment if they take with them items of their furniture that have an emotional attachment. In this situation it is important to understand Martin Buber's dis-

[1] Excerpt from Alexander Miller, *The Renewal of Man* (New York: Doubleday & Co., Inc., 1955), p. 54. Copyright © 1955 by Alexander Miller. Reprinted by permission of Doubleday & Co., Inc.

tinction between an I–Thou relationship and I–It relationship. An I–It relationship is objective and nonpersonal and has a very low meaning level. An I–Thou relationship is highly meaningful, even though it may be with an object. Meaningful objects contribute to our sense of satisfaction.

My invalid brother taught me this lesson. He was highly restricted in his activities and did not get away from the hotel-to-office routine of his life very often. One day we were riding through the countryside. He said, "Even the broomsage looks beautiful to me!" From that time until now, I never see broomsage without thinking of my brother's beautiful life and the way that ordinary things became opportunities of joy for him.

Let me urge you to find some things that seem beautiful to you and hold on to them. Reach out and include more of them. Increase the boundaries of your joy. Tune in to other people. I do not know of one unhappy person who is really interested in other people. Think of that. When we remain interested only in ourselves, we condemn ourselves to a life of unhappiness. We may be in pain. We may have troubles. We may have burdens. We may not have any money. But if we *really* care about other people and invest ourselves in other people and are sensitive to other people, the level of our unhappiness will be sharply reduced. The elevation of our joy will be sharply increased. You can count on that.

One of the most pathetic statements I ever read was written by a woman who had been a widow for twenty years. Her children were grown and scattered. She said, "No one has touched me in twenty years." It was disturbing to think that someone was so isolated from the world as that. I think everyone needs to be hugged from time to time, without violating good judgment or propriety, and to be assured that someone loves them.

If you want to increase the boundaries of your joy, get

interested in other people. Care about them. Increase the scope of your conscious awareness of other people, of things, and do it aggressively.

Above all, keep on keeping on. One of our retired Methodist preachers is in his late seventies. He plays golf several times a week. He regularly defeats other players twenty years younger than he. Now he is building a house! He has a new project going all the time. He is determined to *live* until he dies. Do not let the world close in on you. You do not have to allow it. The greatest freedom you have is the freedom to choose the attitude you will take toward your circumstances.

Overcoming Discouragement

Chances are that each of us has faced discouragement many times. Discouragement seems to accompany all of the other negative emotions. Most of us are dominated by our dreams and expectations. The dreams never seem precisely to reflect reality. The expectations never seem to be fulfilled completely. Thus our task is one of continually learning to settle for less than we had anticipated.

The acids of disappointment eat away at the spirit of persons. Motivation is diminished. Something fine and noble in us dies a little with every discouragement. Nevertheless, we have learned that all of life is a process of dying and renewal. The death of a dream can be the moment of a new beginning, or it can be the beginning of the end. I believe that discouragement is not the end but the beginning of an opportunity.

This belief has not come easily. As a teenager, my greatest ambition was to be one of the starting five of my high school basketball team. As a result of hard work and intense desire, I worked my way to the seventh position. But the coach only used six players!

College was an obstacle course to be endured for the sake of my vocation. Seminary proved to be a disappointment, in retrospect, as I discovered in my ministry that I was by no means prepared to meet the challenge of human need either in the pulpit or in private conversation. Two exhausting attempts to achieve the doctor of philosophy degree were an exercise in ambivalence—extreme desire clashing with the fear that I would not make it. I lived daily with discouragement.

The ultimate success of my efforts produced the proverbial pride before a fall. I experienced a tremendous sense of accomplishment, only to be placed in a vocational situation in which my every effort, every capability, every shred of moral discernment proved ineffectual. I am not yet fully able to determine whether what I did at my lowest point was an act of complete faith or utter despair. I said, "God, if you don't do it, it just won't get done!" Of course, if I had been experiencing total despair, I would not have surrendered my situation to God.

God led me through that difficulty. I received scars and heartbreaks. I suppose there are those who would say, "You should have surrendered it to God sooner." For me that is too simplistic an answer. And I have discovered that to tell someone to turn it all over to God when he or she is overwhelmed with discouragement is to compound the frustration. Sometimes people do not know how to turn things over to God.

We *do* need the realization that God is with us. We *do* need the strength that God alone provides. And sometimes we need to hold on to faith by the fingernails. We can and should live our lives in the awareness that God loves us and cares for us. Faith is neither a Pollyanna retreat from daily reality nor is it the kind of naive egotism that assumes that God is going to reserve for us a parking place on a busy street.

For me, faith is both an act of surrender to God and a context of continual trust in God. Such faith does not preclude discouragement. In fact, it may increase the likelihood of discouragement. The higher our aspirations, the more elevated our hopes; and the nobler our dreams, the more likely is the threat of discouragement. Nevertheless, like discouragement, faith is not the end of something but the beginning of something. Once we have surrendered ourselves to God, it is time to take a new look at what else we can do to ennoble an otherwise dismal situation.

Discouraging situations can be made better. Sometimes they can be changed, but they rarely go away or evaporate. They have to be faced and dealt with—sometimes it seems, unendingly. However, I am often reminded of Goethe's observation that there is no predicament that we cannot ennoble either by doing or by enduring. Rarely is a situation so totally hopeless that absolutely nothing can be done.

Betsy Barton must have been about as discouraged as any person could ever be. She had been paralyzed for six years. Every effort to secure help and healing had proved ineffective. Hope was almost gone. One day her neighbor noticed that she was not breathing properly. "Breathe like this," he said. He also taught her how to exercise her stomach muscles, which she could still use. By learning to breathe properly and exercise her stomach muscles, two things she could still do, she began the road to recovery. She said, "With these two simple things as rungs, I started to climb the ladder of strength to win back my life."

We may not be physically paralyzed, but there may be times when merely to continue breathing seems to require too great an effort. That is the time to remind ourselves that God is good and to hang on to faith with a fierce determination.

In the face of discouragement there are times when we can *do:* do the next thing, take the next step, keep on keeping on. There are other times when we can do for others. It is true that much discouragement arises from our own failures and our own personal circumstances. It is also true that much of our discouragement arises from the failures of others; their apathy, recalcitrance, and incompetence. We must deal with these hard facts realistically without becoming unduly cynical about human behavior on the one hand or unduly optimistic on the other.

This is not to suggest that we merely lower the level of our expectations in order to avoid disappointment. It is to suggest that a highly elevated expectation of the performance or conduct of others is a virtual guarantee of discouragement. We would do well to change the balance of expectation from receiving to giving. When Jesus suggested that he who gives his life ultimately finds it (Mark 8:35), he was pointing to one of the most certain ways to overcome discouragement.

Viktor Frankl describes a young man who throughout a long spell of unemployment, which drove him to despair and almost to suicide . . . experienced only one good hour. One day he was sitting alone in a park and noticed on the next bench a weeping girl. He went over to her and asked her what was the matter. She told him her troubles and declared that she was firmly resolved to commit suicide. The young man summoned up all his powers of persuasion to talk the girl out of her intention, and finally succeeded. That moment—the only moment of joy in a long time and the one bright spot for a long time to come—at last gave back to him the feeling of having a task to face and of being able to accomplish something. And that feeling pulled him out of his apathy, although he was to experience many a backsliding still.[1]

[1] Viktor, Frankl, *The Doctor and the Soul* (New York: Alfred A. Knopf Inc., 1966), p. 124.

We may "talk" more people out of suicide than we ever suspect by the simple act of paying attention to them. Letting them know that they are important and that someone cares about them will not only do them good but also may well reinforce our own reason to exist.

It may be that the ideas suggested have simply added to our own sense of frustration. Certainly trusting God, doing what we can, and being oriented with a giving mentality toward others are helpful suggestions. But they are by no means the whole answer. There are times when we have trusted God as totally as we know how to do, and the situation remains dark and bleak. There are times when we can see nothing else at all that we can do. And there are times when no amount of mental orientation toward others will resolve the lingering doubt that we have done all that we can do.

I can only suggest that in such a time we must simply endure. Sometimes life consists of the effort involved in taking the next step, doing the next thing, existing through the next movement. That is not an exciting possibility, but it does have value. It provides the setting for the ultimate, the final freedom—the freedom to choose our attitude in a given set of circumstances.

Modern psychology describes at least three categories of values. The first category is composed of the creative values that we actualize by doing. The second category consists of those artistic and aesthetic values that emerge in a context of human enjoyment and expression. The third category consists of attitudinal values. Frankl says:

> Attitudinal values, however, are actualized whenever the individual is faced with something unalterable; something imposed by destiny. From the manner in which a person takes these things into himself, assimilates these difficulties into his own psyche, there flows an incalculable multitude of value-potentialities. This means that *human life can be*

fulfilled not only in creating and enjoying, but also in suffering![2]

A tremendous act of will is required to do this, but sometimes discouragement can be prevented from ruling our lives by a firm refusal to allow it to do so! We can find help for our firm resolve in the awareness that God will be with us to replenish our inner strength. St. Paul discovered this in his own life. He said, "We do not lose heart. Though our outer nature is wasting away, our inner nature is being renewed every day" (2 Corinthians 4:16).

In this era of the Bomb, I have to believe that. Since Hiroshima a cosmic discouragement has gripped the world. Those who know the most give me the impression of being the most anxious about the future of civilization as we know it. That is why I am so encouraged by the experience of Jiro Ishii. After the atomic destruction of Hiroshima, Jiro entered the city and searched in vain for his parents. As he left the city, he looked back at a scene of total destruction. There was no sign of life, no foliage, nothing but destruction marked by an ominous silence. On his way out of the city he noticed at the roots of a burned tree stump a small shoot of green. It reminded him of the power of life that is constantly struggling in the face of death and destruction. He went to Hiroshima in despair and left in hope.

We all pray that our world will never again have to face such desolation. Yet when darkness seems total, we can hardly conceive of anything worse. When our world gets dark and we are tempted to give up, we must do all we can. We must do for others all we can. We must endure, hold on, until the light at the other end of the tunnel comes into view. It *will* come into view. The light is still shining in the cosmic darkness, for the darkness has not been able to put it out. *John*

2 *Ibid.*, pp. 105-106.

Creative Anger

Lynn Harold Hough tells of a university president who was often thwarted in his attempt to secure funds by a young professor who constantly blurted out the painful truth. The president invited the young teacher to attend chapel on the day he was to speak. The president talked about the diplomacy of Jesus. He presented Jesus as a master of tact who was always patient and kind in his dealings with people.

The young professor was duly impressed. He expressed his desire to be more diplomatic. The president breathed a complacent sigh of relief. He was a moment premature, however, for in the next breath the professor said, "One thing bothers me. If Jesus was so beautifully diplomatic, how did he ever manage to get himself crucified?"

It is particularly comforting to realize that Jesus did not get along with everybody. Neither was he stoically patient in every situation. There are occasions when he was a good deal less than kind. Jesus threw himself into the caldron of human relationships with an intensity that was all-consuming. That was due to the fact that he had a concern that was all-embracing. He cared what happened to persons—and he cared deeply!

John presents a vivid picture of an angry Christ. He strode deliberately into the temple with a whip in his hands and drove the money changers out. He turned over tables and lashed out in an overt expression of anger. There can be little doubt that he was angry. It may be significant that John places this event at the forefront of Jesus' ministry. What are we to make of this angry Christ? Was he out of character here? Did this act and this emotion reflect the character of God? Was Jesus less divine with a whip in his hands than when those hands were nailed to a cross?

If this event does in fact depict the character of God, we shall have to view the emotion of anger in a new light. It is true that anger has usually been viewed as a base and unlovely element, emerging to becloud the soul at awkward and frustrating moments. Most of us are embarrassed with ourselves when we reflect upon our anger in past situations. We have probably had occasion to be embarrassed by the conduct of a friend at a moment of his or her importune anger in a group or even a crowd. We seldom know how to be angry or how to let another person be angry usefully.

It is not too much to suggest that a great many people live in an atmosphere of subliminal anger most of the time. Some word or phrase, some action or attitude will often trigger an emotion of anger out of all proportion to the incident itself. "That really tees me off" is a conditioned response that has been associated with a series of incidents or experiences that "load" a person in much the same way as one would load a gun. When in those incidents, people are ready to be angry. That is why family life and the entire social context is so volatile. That is why divorces occur and riots break out "for no reason." In such a context it is understandable that there is a strong determination to keep the lid on the emotion of anger.

It is true that most expressions of anger are not only unlovely but also destructive. We may wisely pray to be delivered from destructive anger. Nevertheless, the cleansing of the temple draws us up short and causes us to reconsider the saying that there is no sinful emotion, just sinful uses of emotion. For that reason we must learn to deal with anger creatively.

Anger is not creative when it is unrecognized. Anyone who has ever participated in a sensitivity group is likely to have been put on the defensive by a group member's question, "Why are you so angry?" Sensitivity groups have a way of enabling and allowing persons to vent and expose subliminal or hidden anger. Psychologists often see this venting process as helpful.

Anger is not creative when it is uncontrolled. "Blowing one's top" is probably more destructive than therapeutic. Such anger can be the insertion of deadly poison into the stream of human relationships. Howard Thurman reminds us of the mountain folklore that says that at the particular time of year when the rattlesnake sheds its skin, it remains blind and immobile. At the slightest movement near by, it strikes in the direction of the movement or the sound. If some object touches its body, it strikes the spot that has been touched. Thus it poisons itself with its own venom. To lose one's temper can be a kind of blind striking that does more harm than good.

Witness today the high incidence of hypertension, high blood pressure, heart attacks, and ulcers. Many of these conditions are injuries done to the body by an unchanneled and poisonous anger. There ought to be better ways to defuse this self-destructive bomb than with antacid tablets and tranquilizers. Each of us has probably manifested bodily symptoms of unresolved anger at one time or another.

Anger is not creative when it is unrelated to constructive moral values. Society seems to be victimized more by misguided indignation than by venomous hatreds. There was a time in the early days of movies when cowboys would come to town on Saturdays. On Saturdays the theaters always showed western movies. The plot was always the same: the villian (black hat) would abuse the heroine, and the hero (white hat) would ride to the rescue. The cowboys in the audience would often become so incensed at the situation that they would draw their guns and shoot holes in the projection screen.

In our own time some demonstrations, book burnings, and riots have been characterized by a similar futile action. The participants not only missed the target but could not *find* the target. The destruction was ridiculous as well as tragic. We do not know what to do with our anger! No wonder we are leary of any expression of it! Yet for our own health and the health of our society, we are going to have to learn to view the fact of anger differently and to use it creatively.

We need to realize—and to promulgate the realization—that clean anger is as much a symbol of God's character and will as any other emotion. Love is a beautiful emotion, but it is possible to love destructively. Anger is usually regarded as an ugly, destructive emotion, but it is possible to be angry creatively.

Anger is not necessarily the opposite of love. Sometimes it can be love's clearest and most appropriate expression. We feel deeply about the things that matter most to us. The significant thing is to make certain that the realities which matter most to us personally are also the most important in God's purpose for human life. As someone has so well said, "You can tell the size of a person by the size of the thing it takes to make him or her angry."

Further, we need to stop feeling guilty for our anger. We should feel guilt for those thoughts and actions that violate our responsibility *to* God and our responsibility *for* the well-being of persons. It is inappropriate to feel guilt because of anger that is the result of injustice, the victimization of persons, and the abuse of human dignity.

We can use anger creatively like a purging flame to melt the ice of apathy and neglect. We can use it as a motivating force to correct abuses and injustices. Elie Wiesel, speaking to a large assembly at Emory University, reflected that no human being should have to see or endure the things he had witnessed and endured in several concentration camps during the Nazi era. He pointed out that most of the survivors of those camps were dedicated to making the world free of injustice and atrocities. "That is a miracle," he said. We can be grateful to those who are dedicated to keeping the memory of the holocaust alive in a world that would like to forget it.

We can use anger creatively to ignite the conscience of a community or a nation. Martin Luther King, Jr., was described by many people as a troublemaker and rabble-rouser. My feeling at the time and my considered reflection since is that the trouble was already very much present. Anger seethed in the minds and hearts of black persons. Community after community was on the verge of explosion. Any action of the power structure would have exacerbated the oppression. Dr. King went to these communities with the power of love. He helped black people strengthen their anger collectively, focus their anger on the system rather than on persons, demonstrate their anger in an appeal to the public conscience, and channel their anger into a political revolution resulting in more justice for everyone.

We can use anger creatively to attack a problem. Candy Lightner was devastated by grief at the loss of her thirteen-year-old daughter, killed by a drunken driver. Soon her grief became an intense flame of anger at a system that seemed not only to tolerate drunken drivers but to perpetuate the problem with weak laws and lax enforcement. She organized Mothers Against Drunk Drivers (MADD). This movement has had a tremendous effect in awakening the conscience of our nation and motivating legislators, police officers, and judges to move to address the problem of the driver who is under the influence of alcohol or other drugs.

It is crucial for each of us to realize that we do not need to feel guilty about our anger. We need to recognize it, control it, channel it creatively, and use it to promote the values we have received from the hand of God.

When Anxiety Grips

One of the unforgettable moments of my life occurred on the day I thought I was going to die. I was thirty-two years old. The incident occurred at approximately six o'clock in the morning. I had been studying for twenty-fours hours with only momentary breaks. I was driving from Bowdon, Georgia, to Atlanta to sit for one of the doctoral qualifying examinations when I became aware of increasing pain in my chest. It grew intense. I became dizzy. Perspiration formed on my forehead. My mouth was dry. As I steered the car to the side of the road and stopped, my immediate thought was of death. I felt cheated and disappointed by life. I was also concerned for the welfare of my wife and children.

I sat quietly for a few minutes. The symptoms lessened, and I proceeded to the site of the examination. I sat for the examination under what has come to be regarded as the normal pressures characteristic of the occasion.

In retrospect, I have concluded that I experienced that

day the symptoms of acute anxiety. I also learned that anxiety is normal when it is directly related to either a threat of physical danger or a threat to one's perilously elevated hopes.

Anxiety is the stimulation of the emotional system in the face of a threat. It is different from fear, although the two may go together. The element of fear is always to some degree present in anxiety. Psychologists describe anxiety as the "ambivalence of fear and desire." We are motivated by our desires and frustrated by our fears. When the two are in conjunction, we experience anxiety.

An experience with my young daughter will illustrate the distinction. One day I was teaching her to ride a pony. As she grew more confident, she wanted to ride the pony alone. I thought she was not yet ready and suggested that I run alongside and hold onto the bridle. As the pony began to run, I saw the look on her countenance change from one of delight to one of anxiety. She still wanted the pony to run, but she was increasingly unable to tolerate the threat involved.

When anxiety is the emotional response to the presence of danger, the element of fear will be dominant. Fear is an emotional "spur at the flank of life" that keeps us on the move. When anxiety is the emotional response to our perilously elevated hopes, the element of desire will be dominant. Then anxiety is a kind of stimulant of the spirit, a feeling of anticipation flavored with the fear that we have aimed too high and are riding for a fall.

While it is true that nothing creatively significant would ever be accomplished without this combination of desire and fear, it is also true that anxiety can paralyze, stiffen, and destroy. It can be so excessive a stimulant that we break apart amidst the stresses and strains of daily living. Anxiety may be compared to microscopic cracks in the metal body of an airliner that cause the body to give way under the stresses of turbulence. We may not notice—and others may not notice—our anxieties, but a dissolute personality will surely break under conditions that require wholeness. We are not likely to escape from the conditions that promote anxiety. Our only healthy alternative is to come to the kind of self-understanding in which the balance of fear and desire is a healthy one.

We may identify with the mood suggested by such play titles as *Stop the World, I Want to Get Off* and *Cat on a Hot Tin Roof*. That is due to the fact that our existence in the world is a threatened one. The threats of war, economic deprivation, and illness are obvious. We deal with these rationally and practically as we would deal with any clear and present danger. These overt threats call for overt action. They are a problem, but they can be managed.

There are other threats that make anxiety more of a problem. These threats have to do with our understanding of our selfhood and can cause anxiety to be subliminal, an undercurrent of the stream of life that pulls us under at crucial moments. These threats tend to make life miserable because we do not have the wholeness of selfhood that dealing with these threats requires. They are the threat of meaninglessness, the threat of condemnation, and the threat of finitude. If we are to achieve some measure of victory over the negative aspects of anxiety, we shall have to deal with these interior threats to a satisfying life.

We have come to a better understanding of the threat of meaninglessness as the result of a development in the science of psychology. The first school of psychiatry, under Freud, taught that what is wrong with persons is that they are frustrated by their inability to fulfill their desires. The second school of psychiatry, under Adler, taught that persons are plagued by an inability to adapt to society, to exert power over others. The so-called "third Viennese school" of Viktor Frankl emphasized the premise that persons, in order to achieve emotional health, must find a meaningful place in existence.

The sense of meaninglessness pervades all levels of modern society. Increasing numbers of young people do not seem to have a clear idea either of their own identities or what they want to do with their lives. Middle-aged adults fall apart internally because their images of accomplishment either change frustratingly or evaporate, exposing an illusion. Older adults retire from their jobs and, having attached their "reason-for-living" to their jobs, find themselves with no further real reason to live. Thus, hell begins prematurely.

Jean-Paul Sartre, the French existentialist philosopher, has put his finger upon the human predicament in a play titled *No Exit*. The characters are located in hell. To their amazement, nothing seems to have changed; everything is essentially the same as on earth, except that the discontent vaguely felt on earth grows more intense. Then the discontent becomes intolerable because they realize that it is interminable. One character finally understands: "Hell is—other people!"[1]

I believe that hell is not other people. Hell is oneself endlessly existing without meaning.

A second threat to a satisfying life is a sense of condemnation. This threat is at the root of our tremendous desire to be accepted by our peers. That desire is the source of herd morality and is particularly noticeable in young people who often go to extreme lengths to gain acceptance by their in-group. It is ironic to me that hippies and other counterculture people expressed their rebellion against establishment types of conformity with a more highly visible and more precisely defined pattern of conformity.

Adults may be less visible in their conformity merely

---

[1]Jean-Paul Sartre, *No Exit and Three Other Plays* (New York: Alfred Knopf, Inc., 1955), p. 47.

because their life-style has become "the way things are." This fact simply serves to force the sense of alienation underground. T. S. Eliot, in *The Cocktail Party*, has one of the characters say:

> It's not the feeling of anything I've ever *done*,
> Which I might get away from, or of anything in me
> I could get rid of—but of emptiness, of failure
> Towards someone, or something, outside of myself;
> And I feel I must . . . atone—is that the word?[2]

Such cosmic anxiety is not likely to go away when one has a better understanding of the nature of the predicament or even as a result of identifying specific causes of guilt. The threat is deeper and may have no specific cause that one might correct by retribution or good intentions. It must be dealt with by a reconciliation with the very ground of one's being, with God.

The third interior threat with which we must live is the threat of our finitude. Martin Heidegger, one of the foremost philosophers of our century, came to the conclusion that the awareness that we are creatures who will die dominates the consciousness of modern humanity. That awareness, like an earth tremor, keeps us unsteady. It is not so much that we fear death; we are just uneasy about it.

Blaise Pascal has reminded us that the *fact* of death is less threatening than the *thought* of death when we are not in danger. The real threat is the fact of our finitude. We waste away. In the face of that disarming fact, we fight a fantastic battle to maintain the appearance and the vigor of our prime years. And if we are not paralyzed by such anxiety, we do feel a little stiffened by it.

We can meet the challenge of *exterior* threats by intelligent preparation of one sort or another. Military preparedness, economic planning, and a definite program of

[2]T.S. Eliot, *The Cocktail Party* (New York: Harcourt Brace Jovanovich Inc., 1950), pp. 136-137. Copyright 1950 by T.S. Eliot; renewed 1978 by Isme Valerie Eliot. Reprinted by permission of Harcourt Brace Jovanovich, Inc.

health care will go a long way toward relieving our anxiety in those areas. We meet the challenge of the *interior* threats in a less direct but even more effective way.

The Christian understanding of life speaks plainly to our anxiety. We immediately think of the words of Jesus who said, "Do not be anxious." Those words, taken alone, only serve to increase frustration. But Jesus said, "*Therefore* do not be anxious" (Matthew 6:13a). The "therefore" is of paramount importance. Christianity is a message about the nature of God and the nature of our relationship with God. It tells us who we are; for example, we are made in the image of God. Our dignity, our meaning, our ultimate security derive from God.

To every threat of meaninglessness, Christianity answers with the word "destiny." We have a God-given purpose to our lives. God's invitation to respond to God comes to us filled with possibility. We have an ultimate freedom that no earthly physical restriction can take from us and that is to choose our attitude in a given set of circumstances. This is not fatalism (the view that God causes everything to happen) but faith.

To have faith is to live our lives in the awareness of God's purpose for the world as we see that purpose revealed in Jesus. It is to know that in all the struggles of life, good and bad, God is at work *for* good *with* those who will respond to God's goodness. We need not ever doubt that God is good and that God's goodness is the essential fact characteristic of God's relationship with the world. That is our basic security.

To the threat of condemnation Christianity answers with the word "acceptance." The Christian teaching of salvation by grace is essentially this: God accepts us just as we are. God's acceptance is not based on our merits or qualifications. Paul Tillich expressed this truth with beautiful clarity:

Sometimes at that moment a wave of light breaks into our darkness, and it is as though a voice were saying: "You are accepted. *You are accepted,* accepted by that which is greater than you, and the name of which you do not know. Do not ask for the name now; perhaps you will find it later. Do not try to do anything now; perhaps later you will do much. Do not seek for anything; do not perform anything; do not intend anything. *Simply accept the fact that you are accepted!*"[3]

The full realization that we are accepted by God will dissipate any anxiety of self-condemnation. That awareness of who we are and the nature of our security in God should remove the sting of anxiety from the question of the approval of others. We may still enjoy the approval of others, but the desire for it will no longer be a frantic affair.

To the threat of finitude the Christian understanding of life answers with the word "victory." The resurrection of Jesus Christ did not eliminate the fact of death, but it did remove the sting of death. We still die. We still have only a limited time in which to do our work. Our bodies still fade. But while the outer nature is fading away, the inner nature is being renewed every day.

The Christian witness to resurrection is not meant to say that there is no death. Our finitude takes on a different meaning. We face that darkness of death with the same confidence as one who knows he or she has a light. Darkness is not a terror to one who knows he or she has a light that will never go out. We have such a light in Jesus Christ. We can know that God intends our eternal well-being. To know that fact changes our attitudes about everything.

[3] Paul Tillich, *The Shaking of the Foundations* (New York: Charles Scribner's Sons, 1948). p. 162.

Consulting the Eyes of God

The context of confusion in which the fact of human suffering is considered makes suffering more of a problem than it needs to be. Many persons seem to assume that if God would just "say the word," suffering would cease to exist. This is especially true in individual cases in which it is assumed that the prayer of faith will persuade God to "say the word" and end a particular person's suffering by healing his or her body.

The confusion is compounded by the influence of that strand of Christian thought that rejoices in suffering. Paul found his strength "made perfect in weakness" (2 Corinthians 12:9). He identified his sufferings with Christ and counted them as an opportunity (Romans 8:17 and Philippians 1:29). This determination of Paul to endure the necessary pain resulting from the conflicts of a disciple has translated the pain into a badge of discipleship itself; the Christian is one who suffers.

A third aspect of our confusion is the assumption that

"God will not put more on us than we can bear." That is, suffering comes from God. Such thinking assumes that God either wills suffering or allows it. Each of us has heard some variant of the consoling efforts of the young prince to the spastic boy: "You must be God's favorite pupil. He gave you the hardest problem."

It doesn't help very much to try to resolve the problem by concluding that in some ultimate and mysterious way, suffering is a good thing. It is true that many persons have come through the caldron of pain to a stronger character and a more radiant faith than they had. We can appreciate Paul's statement, "Suffering produces endurance, and endurance produces character, and character produces hope" (Romans 5:3,4). These good results only serve to increase the total confusion about suffering itself and make it more of a problem of faith and understanding than it needs to be.

Suffering is a problem because it is an agonizing fact of human experience. It is *more* of a problem because of our inferences about it. Ivan, in Dostoyevsky's *The Brothers Karamazov*, observes that if God has offered man suffering as a pass through life, he for one must respectfully return the ticket. Good for Ivan!

Most of the negative emotions dealt with in this book are interwoven in the broad fabric of suffering. I do not claim in this brief section to be able to dissipate the fog of confusion that has so thoroughly beclouded the human scene with regard to suffering. But I had a deep, personal struggle with this question for a long time. I have seen one thing clearly, and for me, this one insight was like the heat of the sun burning through the chill early morning fog to warm my spirit: *God does not intend our suffering.*

When I face the ultimate questions of life, I am thankful for what I have learned from my family. I have learned that the problem of suffering far outweighs the fact of pain.

Suffering, for me, was a personal problem long before it became a theological problem.

As a child I saw my father struggle with the problem of vocational humiliation. He had risen through the ranks to an executive sales position with the Georgia Power Company. During the economic depression of the early 1930s he lost his job with the company. He returned to the small town in which he had been reared, fell back on the skills he had learned "on the way up," accepted the largesse of his wife's family, and became the town plumber.

Only as an adult was I able to comprehend something of the cost of that sequence of events to my father's spirit. He was forced by circumstances to return home and become a general flunky in order to provide for his family. I can remember him and other men gathering at a local automobile service station every afternoon. I gradually realized that they had no work, and it was a matter of male pride not to be around the house during working hours!

I learned from my father to engage in one's vocation with pride, even when displacement threatens humiliation. I sensed that human dignity may increase one's suffering in humiliating circumstances. Nevertheless, human dignity is the only thing that can lift one *above* those circumstances.

In later years a malignant tumor developed on my father's esophagus. I saw him bear his pain with equanimity and without self-pity. He died in surgery. His conduct and demeanor were such that I never dreamed he was looking death in the face.

I am thankful that I learned from my mother how to bear the suffering of economic deprivation. She taught me how to endure economic depression with dignity. We became poor because there was no money, but we were never impoverished. I never realized what our economic situation was because my mother bore her deprivation without complaining. It *was* a deprivation because her life had been characterized by affluence. Her unwillingness to succumb to self-pity saved her children from being victimized by insecurity and created in us a capacity to deal with adversity.

I learned from my brother how to deal with the suffering of physical incapacitation. From my earliest recollection he was in a wheelchair. Every part of his body was skeletonized except his face. He could not move any part of his body except his head and his hands. Every aspect of his physical care had to be done for him, or prepared so that he could do it himself. For example, he brushed his teeth by moving his head from side to side after his body had been postured and the brush placed in his hand. Bruce learned his limits early and worked within them.

With the assistance of many friends who attended to his needs, Bruce graduated in 1940 from the University of Georgia. It took him two years to find a job, and only then was he hired because so many able-bodied men were away at war. He became an excellent newspaperman, and finally associate editor of the Columbus (Georgia) *Ledger*. He died at thirty-two of muscular dystrophy.

Three days before his death, Bruce wrote an editorial about the plans of B'nai B'rith to do research on muscular dystrophy, which he called "a disease as hopeless as cancer in its last stages." He said, "There is no retreat from it save death . . . only the most intensive laboratory effort will rip the shroud from the killer's secrets . . . the appalling lack of interest in this most hopeless of diseases is not a cheering thought." Two days later Bruce called for our father to take him home. He died that night—the above-mentioned words being the closest he ever came to a complaint.

I was eleven years younger than Bruce. My training for the Christian ministry was an intense concern to him. His most memorable advice to me was, "Don't ever assume, Garnett, that the world owes you a living." Whenever misfortune befalls me or someone close to me and I hear (or am tempted to ask) "Why me?" I remember with gratitude the lessons of raw courage I learned from my brother. There was a wide variation of theological viewpoints among these members of my family. For the most part, they were not aware of being theologically oriented. Somewhere along the way, however, *they had refused to attribute the vicissitudes of life to the purposes of God.* They refused to give in to that narrow fatalism (God wills everything that happens) that loses sight of the goodness of God when the foggy mists of suffering shut out the horizons of hope.

I confess that these observations about members of my family were not clearly conceptualized as I was growing up. At best they were on the periphery of my consciousness. The impressions were there, nevertheless. It was much later that I was able to develop a theological understanding of these lessons of faith and fortitude. For this I am thankful to God for my teachers. They all contributed significantly to my thinking. Of course, they are too many to mention by name. Let me mention three of them who are responsible for specific insights.

I am thankful for Carl Michalson. He drove home the tremendously liberating point that God does not intend our suffering. The awareness of this lifted the fog of confusion for me. God is not the creator of suffering. The suffering with which God is involved is the suffering God encounters in efforts to reach out the hand of forgiveness and love to a rebellious world and a malignant nature. When we identify with God's suffering in and through Jesus, we see God not as a part of the problem but as a part of the solution. Jesus *never* brought pain. His intention was *always* for healing. God struggles with something alien and demonic that resists God's purposes. We are caught up in the struggle, and we share the pain. It is only as we realize that it is a *shared* pain that we can "rejoice in suffering." That is what all those biblical references to suffering with Christ mean to me.

Michalson once described an experience that proved very illuminating to me. In his relationship with his young son, he would often engage in horseplay and general scuffling. Sometimes it would get rough. Pain would ensue. He noticed that when the pressure on his son would become painful, his son would steal a quick look at his father's eyes to determine whether he and his dad were still frolicking or whether he was feeling the firm hand of punishment. If the son saw merriment and approval, the pain constituted no crisis for him. When we look into the face of Jesus amidst the vicissitudes of life, our pain still hurts, but it is not a crisis because we do not see that God intends our suffering.

It was Michalson who suggested that I do my doctoral research in the same area as the work of his teacher, Edwin Lewis. Lewis helped me to work through the speculative efforts to explain suffering. These usually got no farther than the textbook dilemma: either God is good but weak or he is strong but evil (the creator of evil). In his book *The Creator and the Adversary*, Lewis takes seriously, if not literally, the biblical symbolism of Satan and the devil. He faces the fact that God is dealing redemptively with evil, whether it be sin and the results of sin in the world or whether it be malignant resistance to or perversion of God's creative purpose. Lewis says:

> To know, not that God creates the evil but hates it, to know that it rises up against him as it does against us, to know that its conquest is a problem for him as it is for us, to know that it will yield, if it yield at all, not to a gesture of omnipotence but to the steady persistence of suffering love—to know this is not to change anything in the character of the human situation.
>
> Something, nevertheless, is changed. The *approach* to the situation is changed. There is a change in the *resources* avail-

able for meeting it. There is a change in the ultimate expectation. If there is a Love that will not let men go, despair and pessimism will be done away.[4]

This by no means resolves every intellectual and emotional problem having to do with human suffering. But it caused the breakthrough that enabled me to see whose side God was on. We may never resolve the metaphysical questions. But we can know the intention of God.

That is why I am thankful for Claude Thompson. He had studied with Edwin Lewis. He and Michalson were theologically far apart. Yet the application of their faith to the circumstances of life was victorious in each case. I learned that Dr. Thompson had cancer. I went to his office where he continued to work after the diagnosis and subsequent surgery. When I asked him about his physical condition, he replied, "I am going to be all right." Several months later a friend sent me a copy of a sermon that Dr. Thompson had preached to the theological student body on the subject of his imminent death. It was a calm and victorious statement of faith. His suffering and death were no crisis for him. *He had consulted the eyes of God!*

I have not thought that these reflections would solve the problem of suffering for you. Suffering is infinitely varied and intensely personal. You may need many more answers to assuage your doubts. I have studied other answers also, but I have found this to be the hinge on which hope turns for me. Suffering is not going to go away. We must deal with it. As Michalson says: "To know that our suffering is not in *God's* purpose—whatever else may be true of it—is to give us the spiritual grounds for equanimity in suffering."[5] This changes everything.

---

[4]Edwin Lewis, *The Creator and the Adversary* (Nashville: Abingdon Press, 1948), p. 21.
[5]Carl Michalson, *A Faith for Personal Crises* (New York: Charles Scribner's Sons, 1958), p. 153.

Make a Friend
of Your Fear

It is not too much to say that our era of history is made
unsteady by the swirling currents of fear. Russia and the
United States are expending tremendous amounts of their
resources in military buildups as a result of their fear of
each other. Unconsciously the uneasy dread of the Bomb
or radioactive contamination plays a large part in our responses to other nations and to our country's development. The revolution of the world's poor from centuries
of servility makes the leaders of oppressive govenments
uneasy and more reactive. Violent crime makes a jungle of
every dark city street in the United States. Underlying all
of our reactions is a kind of unnamed anxiety, tormenting
minds, sapping strength, and straining at our nerves.

Merril Abbey has said, "While it is true that we are afraid
because the times are dangerous, it is also true that the
times are dangerous because we are afraid."[1] We see signs

[1] Merrill R. Abbey, *Preaching to the Contemporary Mind* (Nashville: Abingdon
Press, 1963), p. 24.

51

of this every day as frightened people barter away their freedoms in the name of security.

Possibly our greatest need is to distinguish between rational fears on the one hand and irrational fears on the other. Carl Michalson observed, "A hunter facing a lion in the African jungles with his gun jammed has a right to be afraid. But if a grown man retreats in dread at the sight of a common cat, something is clearly wrong."[2] Michalson reports a conversation among "three girls arguing about going out in a canoe. One girl refused to go. 'Why?' 'Because I can't swim,' she said. 'But the water here never gets over your knees!' the others countered. 'I still won't go!' she said."[3] When fear grips us, even though there may be some external justification for our caution, our responses often become irrational. Such an irrational response can only be destructive. It preys upon us as individuals and on our society as a whole.

In his book, *The Conquest of Fear*, Basil King says:

> When I say that during most of my conscious life I have been a prey to fears, I take it for granted that I am expressing the case of the majority of people. I cannot remember the time when a dread of one kind or another was not in the air. In childhood it was the fear of going to bed. . . . Later it was the fear of school. . . . Later still . . . the experience . . . of waking in the morning with a feeling of dismay at what we have to do on getting up. . . . Fear dogs one of us in one way and another in another, but everyone in some way.[4]

There was a time when Christian preaching was predominantly fear-oriented. It is ironic that during the last century religion has largely dropped the appeal to fear while

[2] Carl Michalson, *Faith for Personal Crises* (New York: Charles Scribner's Sons, 1958), p. 16.
[3] *Ibid.*, p. 35.
[4] Excerpt from Basil King, *The Conquest of Fear* (New York: Doubleday & Co. Inc., 1921), pp. 1-2. Copyright © 1921 by Doubleday & Co., Inc. Reprinted by permission of Doubleday & Co., Inc.

other human interest groups have begun to emphasize it. One of the more blatant examples of this is in advertising. I saw several runs of a television commercial by a leading automobile tire manufacturer. The commercial presented a woman driving through a deserted area. Her car has a flat tire, and she must stand there alone while scary sounds reverberate around her. In another instance a man points out that her tire is dangerously thin. Then the commerical proceeds to have her worry her way through the desolate countryside. The advertisers in this case were adept in capitalizing upon the element of fear.

Fear is a consuming emotion. It can erode the fibers of our faith and destroy the substance of our motivation. Irrational fear can subvert and destroy all the securities in our society. We must learn how to deal with it! Many books dealing with the problem of fear are negative and unrewarding reading because they assume that all fear is harmful and must be driven out. While it is true that the Bible speaks of perfect love casting out fear, the Bible also strongly indicates that there is such a thing as healthy fear—the fear of the Lord, for example. The term "fear of the Lord" indicates reverence for God, awareness of the awesome holiness of God and our responsibility to God.

The capacity for fear is God-given. It is indigenous to our natures. This fact iş obvious in animal life. In animals the capacity to fear and the added impetus it gives to their escape mechanisms may have enabled them to survive as a species. Fear stimulates additional glandular secretion that enhances muscular capacity. This is true whether the muscles are used for combat or for escape. Thus fear becomes what Michalson called a "spur at the flank of life."[5]

This spur must have been effective for the countryman who encountered a ghost while walking through a cemetery. In reporting the incident the countryman said, "When

[5]Michalson, *Faith for Personal Crises*, p. 15.

I reached out to touch him, he warn't there, and when he reached out to touch me, I warn't there!"

Human survival may well depend upon a healthy use of fear. We must learn a healthy fear of destructive things: dangerous drugs, speeding automobiles, atomic weapons buildup, and other threats to safety and health. In Herman Melville's novel *Moby Dick*, Chief Mate Starbuck exclaims, "I will have no man in my boat who is not afraid of a whale."[6] We recognize that some things are dangerous, and therefore we are not ready to dispense with constructive fear in the structure of society.

When President Franklin Roosevelt said in his first inaugural address that we have nothing to fear but fear itself, he was surely referring to the destructive, irrational fears that can consume us. But we do not have to fear fear. We can make a friend of it. We can use it constructively, letting it become a spur to human survival and human betterment. We need not heed the admonition of Aristophanes to throw fear to the wind. We can grasp it like a sword, not by the blade but by the handle.

We can use fear constructively as a spur to greater understanding. Acceptance of the fact of fear and the God-given capacity for fear opens avenues of increased understanding in our relationships with individual persons and with nations. If we can understand the dominant fears of a nation's people, we will surely know better how to deal with them in a creative manner. It is a liberating experience to be able to have empathy with the fears of another person. We may be saved from the assumption that that person is strange, unfriendly, or dangerous. The context of a relationship is changed when we can enter into an awareness of what the other person is experiencing.

We can use fear constructively as a spur to greater

[6]Herman Melville, *Moby Dick* (New York: Harcourt Brace Jovanovich Inc.,) p. 104.

knowledge. One of the things humans fear most is the unknown. Why not allow this fear to send us with vigor to the test tube and the experiment station? We can thank God for the fear of disease that has set persons to work in thousands of research laboratories, for the fear of hunger that has forced persons to develop increasingly more effective methods of conservation of resources, and for the fear of destruction that has driven individuals, corporations, and nations to greater technological development. It now remains to use these capacities for human benefit rather than for destruction.

We can use fear constructively as a spur to enhanced moral goodness. We properly fear the collapse of moral fiber in our world. When this happens, chaos and destruction follow as a matter of course. We do well to fear the dissolution of family life, increased greed and impersonality in our economic life, and rampant promiscuity in our sex life.

The fear that you will miss the mark and fail to fulfill the creative purpose that God has for you as a unique being in the world, and the fear that you will fail to express clearly enough your own faith in God promote a healthy respect for and a dedicated response to God.

Everything depends upon how we relate to others. That depends upon how we view them. This is clearly reflected in the story of a man who saw a being in the distance. He was consumed with fear because he perceived it to be a dangerous animal. As it came closer, he saw it to be a man. His fear increased because he assumed the man to be an enemy. It was only as they were close together that he recognized the man to be his own brother! You and I can make a difference in the world by the degree to which we refuse to allow fear to determine our perceptions.

Overcoming Boredom

I stood in the Mamertine prison, located near the ancient Roman forum in Rome, Italy. The prison was nothing more than a small room carved out of solid rock. My imagination reached back to the time when the apostle Paul was kept in this place. "Kept" is the word, for it was hardly more than a cage.

Can you imagine Paul the apostle in prison in Rome? He was surrounded by cold stone walls. His life was very likely at an end. Alien soldiers guarded him. There were no rehabilitation programs, libraries, or workshops to help him pass the time. His small body shriveled further for lack of exercise. His mind was poisoned with bitterness and cynicism because of his loneliness and all the sufferings he had experienced. He was bored with the oppression of the nothingness to which his life had come.

Is that the way it was? Not at all! The physical surroundings were as I have described them, but he was not bored or bitter! Instead, his mind leaped the distance to Philippi and he wrote to the Philippians a stirring letter of love and joy. In his mind he joined with the struggles of the churches of Asia, and he wrote to them letters of clarification of the faith.

While in prison Paul was a dynamo of awareness. His mind reached back to all the places he had been, to the needs and concerns of the people who were important to him. He did what he could within the limitations of his confinement. Paul's mind also reached forward, transcending prison walls and the drab nothingness of his surroundings to the vision of a witness to be made in Spain.

Paul apparently died with that vision in his mind and that desire in his heart. There is no reason to believe that Paul was ever bored. Indeed, if I were to define boredom it would be characterized by a *lack* of vision and the *absence* of desire. Paul discovered the Christian way to be a faith that helps to overcome boredom precisely because it gives a vision and a continued motivation.

Never before have persons needed this help as we do in this century. Teilhard de Chardin wrote: "The great enemy of the modern world, 'Public Enemy No. 1,' is *boredom*. . . .I repeat: despite all appearances, Mankind is bored. Perhaps this is the underlying cause of all our troubles. We no longer know what to do with ourselves."[1]

Any one of us will realize that what Father Teilhard says is true merely by reading the faces of the people we encounter on the street, at work, at home, and in church. Watch the boredom mirrored on the faces of those who crowd the stores in aimless shopping wanderings. Watch people fall apart over the weekend when they do not have their regular routine to hold them together. Watch in amazement as marriages collapse as a result of pure boredom.

[1] Teilhard de Chardin, *The Future of Man*, trans. Norman Denny (New York: Harper & Row Publishers, Inc.), pp. 150-151.

Erich Auerbach, in a comment on Flaubert's *Madame Bovary*, captures in one scene the destructive power of boredom:

> The two are sitting at table together; the husband divines nothing of his wife's inner state; they have so little communion that things never even come to a quarrel, an argument, an open conflict. Each of them is so immersed in his own world—she in despair and vague wishdreams, he in his stupid philistine self-complacency—that they are both entirely alone. . . .[2]

This situation expresses what Auerbach calls "unconcrete despair." It is a situation in which nothing in particular happens, "but that nothing has become a heavy, oppressive, threatening something."[3] That oppressive something is boredom.

Spanish-speaking people have a word, *gregueria*, which means "to be bored is to kiss death." The French word *ennui* describes a state of existence in which motivation and caring have been reduced to a minimum, either voluntarily or unconsciously.

The German philosopher Schopenhauer observed that the most general survey shows us that the two foes of human happiness are pain and boredom. As we have become increasingly capable of relieving physical pain and the most burdensome aspects of manual labor, boredom becomes a greater problem. Increased availability of leisure time intensifies the question of what to do with it. Nevertheless, it would be a mistake to assume that boredom can be overcome merely by filling our time. The effort to do this creates another problem, a sense of futility.

Jean-Paul Sartre has shown how this awareness of futility bubbles to the surface of our consciousness no matter how frenzied our activity. Roquentin, in Sartre's novel *Nausea*, illustrated how this happens:

[2] Erich Auerbach, *Mimesis* (Princeton: Princeton University Press, 1953), p. 489.
[3] *Ibid.*, p. 488.

When I found myself on the Boulevard de la Redoute again nothing was left but bitter regret. I said to myself: Perhaps there is nothing in the world I cling to as much as this feeling of adventure; but it comes when it pleases; it is gone so quickly and how empty I am once it has left. Does it, ironically, pay me these short visits in order to show me that I have wasted my life?[4]

I can see no way to resolve the problem of boredom so long as one is plagued with the recurrent suspicion that one has wasted his or her life. The Christian understanding of life before God can help us to deal creatively with the problem of boredom.

First of all, Christ draws us out of ourselves so that we are willing to overcome the walls that hold us in.

No one had more walls to hold her in than did Helen Keller. She was totally blind. She was completely deaf. She lived every day of her life in utter darkness and total silence. Speech for her was an exercise in agonizing futility. By all odds she should have lived an isolated existence of consummate boredom.

Yet Helen Keller broke through those walls to become a gifted writer, religious leader, and radiant example of a remarkable inner strength, joy, and serenity. The major difference between many of us and Helen Keller is that we have physical advantages and she had none. Helen Keller had one other great asset. She had a friend who cared enough about her to bring her out of isolation and to warm her heart with the heart of God. We can have that also. Jesus is a friend who cares enough about us to bring us out of isolation. He can put us in touch with his world in a new and adventuresome way.

A second reason that our faith may help us overcome boredom is that Christ gives us the strength to gain control

[4]Jean-Paul Sartre, *Nausea*, The New Classics Series (New York: James Laughlin, 1938), p. 78. Copyright © 1964 by New Directions Publishing Corporation. Translated by Lloyd Alexander, All Rights Reserved. Reprinted by permission of New Directions.

of our own minds. Goethe said, "He who is firm in will molds the world to himself."

Thought conditioners do help. The power of positive thinking can transform a person's attitudes. Christ gives us the awareness that we can change and he gives us the strength to make the change.

Finally, our Christian faith never lets us retire. The business community has a basic rule of success: Find a need and fill it. Every Christian has his or her working and marching orders. He or she never retires. He or she never needs to feel useless. His or her marching orders extend right on into eternity. We can live the rest of our lives with enthusiasm.

Begin now to look for a need and look for ways in which *you* can do something to help fill that need. Take the first step. Make the first move of friendship and service. You *can* do something. You will be glad that you did.

Don't Die on Friday

I once heard Dr. William Self, pastor of the Wieuca Road Baptist Church in Atlanta, Georgia, give this striking admonition: "Don't die on Friday—your body will rot before they find you on Monday." His warning became vividly real to me when I read the news accounts of the discovery of actor William Holden's decomposed body in his apartment. Dr. Self was referring to a new kind of isolation that plagues urban dwellers today. A person may work from Monday through Friday and then simply disappear until the following Monday. Apartment dwellers may have no personal contacts close enough to bridge the weekend gap. This fact emphasizes what Rollo May predicted would become an increasingly serious urban problem, the problem of loneliness.

Loneliness can be a particularly agonizing kind of hell. Merrill Abbey tells of a woman who jumped to her death from the eleventh floor of a Chicago office building. The suicide note that she left described her anguished state of mind. She wrote, "I'm so alone!" The woman's situation was all too typical of untold thousands of people. She worked at a routine job, had a few occasional friendly contacts, saw a lot of movies, and attended mass on Sunday. A sympathetic coroner's jury report said, "She was past her prime. She was alone. What else could she do?"[1] T. S. Eliot has imaginatively captured the scene:

> One thinks of all the hands
> That are raising dingy shades
> In a thousand furnished rooms.[2]

Although the simile may be dated, the sense of isolation is nevertheless strong. Today the mood may be expressed in terms of all the hands that are turning television dials in a thousand cubicle apartments. The irony of our situation is that we have more persons crowded closer together than ever before and we have become what David Riesman called "the lonely crowd."

Loneliness is no respecter of persons. It is a problem in every age group. Often a child will complain, "I don't have anybody to play with." A preoccupied parent will respond by pointing to a pile of inanimate objects called toys, and the generation gap begins. The child wants the warmth of a friend, and parents give him or her a substitute. On the other hand, it is sometimes counterproductive to provide two friends. Two children may play together well, but a third child is often excluded and the problem occurs again.

A similar sense of being excluded characterizes teenage loneliness. Teenagers are particularly introspective, and the experience can be devastating. I have the feeling that the loneliest place for a teenager to be is in front of a mirror. The ego-diminishing self-analysis might go something like this: "My complexion is bad." "My chin is too sharp." "My ears stick out." "My nose is crooked." Few teenagers can stand before a mirror and not find something wrong. With

[1]Merrill R. Abbey, *Preaching to the Contemporary Mind* (Nashville: Abingdon Press, 1963), p. 116.

[2]T.S. Eliot, "Preludes," *Collected Poems 1909–1962* (New York: Harcourt Brace Jovanovich Inc., 1963), p. 13. Copyright 1936 by Harcourt Brace Jovanovich, Inc.; copyright © 1963, 1964 by T.S. Eliot. Reprinted by permission of the publisher.

this kind of self-analysis taking place, it is understandable that teenagers seem to have a desperate need to be accepted by their peers. Much of the teenage sense of isolation arises from the difficulty of establishing a way to overcome the awkwardness and insecurity involved in relating to other persons. Cliques develop as teenagers get together in a desperate effort not to be left out. Yet someone always is.

Perhaps the greatest loneliness of all is that over-the-hill feeling when one's self-worth is thrown into question in older age. In a depersonalized, highly competitive society that older age may arrive at forty-five or fifty! One's vocation, body, friends, one's whole context of existence can make him or her feel isolated.

This is powerfully illustrated in Ernest Hemingway's *The Old Man and the Sea*. Hemingway vividly portrays a man whose reason for being, his whole life, lies in his vocation. He is a fisherman. He does not merely fish for a living. *He is a fisherman.* His body, his skill, his memories, his anticipations, his satisfactions, all are inseparable from his all-consuming vocation.

Santiago is an *old* man. His body, though strong, gives him reason to wonder whether he is capable of vanquishing a truly big fish. His luck is gone; he has been eighty-five days without a catch. He can sense the silence of the villagers who do not want to be identified with his failure. His one source of emotional sustenance is a small boy whom he taught to fish and who has been his constant companion. Now the boy is prevented from associating with him because the old man is regarded as unlucky.

Everything depends upon a good catch soon. The old man makes elaborate preparations. He uses the best of his skill and experience. He carefully checks the bait, the line, the boat, everything. He goes farther out than before. He fishes at several depths, planning, calculating, thinking all of the time.

When the strike is made, the old man craftily waits until precisely the correct moment to set the hook. Then the battle is joined! For two days and two nights the great fish runs, pulling the boat farther and farther from land. The old man is determined not to be defeated though his hands are cramped and cut and his body begins to weaken. The struggle is of body, mind, and soul, and the old man's admiration for the great fish soars. Nevertheless, the old man *must* win. He is a fisherman!

When finally the weakened fish rises to the surface, the old man draws it in and lashes it to the boat. He realizes that he will never get it to the shore. "I came too far out," he says to himself.

All through the struggle the old man has wished for the boy to be present. It is more than the loneliness of the vigil. It is the loneliness of the struggle, the lack of the sustenance of a friend, and the recurring doubts that his body will serve him well.

The journey home is a struggle in despair. He has no compass, only the instincts of a fisherman. He gets his bearings by the stars and sails resolutely for home. The sharks, attracted by the blood of the great fish, begin to attack. The old man fights the sharks with all the weapons at his disposal. Finally there is nothing left with which to fight, and the fish is mutilated by the sharks. Santiago can no longer bear to see the magnificent creature so totally skeletonized.

Now he has no thought, no pride of the catch, only total weariness, sadness that the splendid fish has been destroyed, and determination to reach home. The old man can sense the dim glow on the horizon before he can see it. He does finally see it and sails for shore with no particular sense of relief. When he reaches shore, he lifts the

mast from the boat and carries it across his back—a cruci-
form. He stumbles, exhausted, to his cabin.

The boy finds the old man and rejoices that he has made
a great catch. To him, it does not matter that the fish is
mutilated. The catch means that the old man's luck has
returned and they can be friends again. He nourishes the
old man. They make plans. The boy has a new resolution
to learn from the old man, but consummate loneliness has
taken its toll. Santiago sleeps the sleep of lethargy and
dreams the dreams of the old.

This is the time that is worst of all in life: when the body
fails embarrassingly; when the vocation is gone; and when
one wonders whether he or she will make the far shore
with the substance of his or her life intact as the sharks of
social and economic circumstances tear away at the sum
total of the investment of one's life. The most profound
insecurity is to wonder whether one's resources will last
until death: "Will I be helpless?" "Will I be penniless?"
"Can I make it until the end?"

I believe the Christian faith can speak helpfully and constructively to the problem of loneliness. Christ tells us who
we are and where we stand in relation to God. In my experience I have related to hundreds of physically and eco-
nomically decimated persons who have been victorious over
loneliness through their faith. Almost every one of them
has referred to the Twenty-Third Psalm as his or her favorite biblical passage. These people have understood the
solitude of the shepherd. They have understood even more
what it is like to go through the valley of the shadow of
death without any fear of evil. They know the sustaining
presence of God.

I want to suggest three things that can make a profound
difference in overcoming loneliness. First, we need to become aware that we are watched over. The psalmist de-
rived immeasurable strength from his awareness of the

presence of God in his life. When he said, "The Lord is my shepherd," he was saying a great deal. At the least, it was an expression of his awareness that he was not alone, that he could feel secure in the tender care of another, and that in some way his basic needs would be met. The writers of the psalms were familiar with overwhelming difficulty. One has only to note the opening lament of Psalm Twenty-Two. Yet the sense of the strengthening and abiding presence of God, if not immediately felt, then at least remembered, is sufficient and reassuring.

A certain town was threatened when the Mississippi River was at flood stage. The men of the town worked diligently to strengthen the levies that protected the town. At night the women would look out from their houses and see the light of the lanterns on the levies. They were reassured by the awareness that they were being watched over. In our time, no person need ever face alone the ultimate loneliness as long as he or she can remember the abiding presence of God.

Second, we need to be reminded that we are loved. Robert Louis Stevenson, who lived with the isolation of illness, observed that we are really indispensable as long as there is someone who loves us. It is true! Each of us is unique. We contribute to the well-being of others by the uniqueness of our being in the world. Sometimes people love us in spite of our bad moments and negative responses. Think how much more they might love us if we were to respond in more positive ways! The most positive way we can respond is to take note of our friends and give value to them.

We can combat loneliness by taking positive action: *We can love.* It is important to keep in mind that one reason we are lonely is that we spend our time commiserating with ourselves in negative and self-defensive terms. "We don't have anybody to play with!" We can *take the initiative* to reach out to other persons, and we can do so in ways that will be helpful to both ourselves and them.

Viktor Frankl reminds us of the one freedom that no person or circumstances can take from us. That is the freedom to choose what one's attitude or response will be. "Affliction does so color life," said a sympathizer to a crippled woman. "Yes," she replied, "and I propose to choose the color." We *can* choose our responses to situations. In that sense we can choose not to be lonely. The first step is to be aware. The second step is an act of will. The third step is the physical act of reaching out to another person.

Overcoming the Questions of Futility

Futility always follows the other emotions, but it is not the last word. Unless one deals with the questions of futility, however, futility can become the last word. I do admit that I am a bit chagrined that the one book of the Bible named "The Preacher" (i.e., Ecclesiastes) begins on a note of futility. We should have a more positive word.

Possibly every age has had its philosophy of despair, but our twentieth century appears to be especially replete with agonized questioners of man's fate. They are those who search—sometimes desperately, sometimes cynically—for God and do not find God. They question the meaning of life, not because they are looking for a meaning but because they have already despaired of finding any meaning. In the past these persons have often been the idle rich or the frustrated malcontents of society. More recently they have been called hippies or existentialists.

In the past such questions were most often raised by a rather well-marked group. Today these questions permeate the very fabric of our society. It may well be that we have asked ourselves these questions. If we haven't already, we will.

My wife and two daughters were traveling with me in Italy a few years ago. We each brought back a memento of the trip. Their gift to me, which they purchased in Rome's famous flea market, was a highly realistic replica of a human skull! They gave it to me because of an incident I had described many times. In a certain bookstore that specialized in used books, a prankster had placed a stack of twenty books. These books, gathering dust, unwanted and unread, were the sole remaining production of a great mind. On top of the stack of books, the prankster had placed a human skull (suggestive of that of the author). At the base of the stack he had placed a small white card with the words *"cui bono"* neatly printed on it. Symbolically the skull had once housed the author's mighty brain. Now it grinned in a ghoulish post-mortem joke, asking in the Latin phrase: "What's the use?"

A person can work all of his or her life to produce books for the betterment of the human condition, only to have them gather dust in the window of some used-books store. A young minister can assume his duties in a church and attempt to apply the teachings of Jesus as best he understands them. He may then discover that sometimes the very people upon whom he must depend do not by any means intend to follow the teachings of Jesus. On the other hand, a young layperson may wish to assume some creative and adventurous tasks in the church or community, only to discover that her major obstacle is the minister. Any one of us may struggle to make a significant contribution to our world, only to discover that there is a good deal of truth to the adage: "You can't fight city hall."

If anyone ever had ample reason to ask herself or himself, "What's the use?" and settle down to a life of innocuous mediocrity, it was the man who was defeated and frustrated at every turn for the great majority of his life. As a young man he was forced to educate himself. Formal schooling was not a viable alternative. As a young lawyer he ran for his state legislature and was defeated. His business failed, and he spent many years paying the debts of an unscrupulous partner. The girl with whom he was deeply in love died. He was finally elected to the United States Congress, but he was defeated after only one term. He had so little influence that he could not even secure a government job. He was defeated in a bid to become elected to the United States Senate. He was defeated in his attempt to become vice-president; and he had the supreme ill fortune to be elected president at the precise time when this·nation was tearing itself apart in civil strife. Yet today Abraham Lincoln's life stands as a symbol of the grand fact that a person's life can amount to something if he or she dares to rise to the challenge of his or her defeats. Any person might well adopt Lincoln's motto: "I will prepare myself—and perhaps my time will come."

Of course, we may be tempted to suggest that, after all, Lincoln stands as one of the giants of our history. He could hardly be considered as a typical model for our thinking today. Besides our society is much too complex for an individual to make any real headway in the face of the mass movements, the manipulative propaganda, and the social forces of our time. It we are thinking this, we are really raising the second question of futility: "What can one solitary life accomplish?"

There is certainly every reason to ask that question in the face of the frustrations we daily encounter. It does appear that one person can't seem to make much headway in changing the direction of a corporate or governmental bureaucracy. The depersonalization of urban life appears to stretch apathy over a city like a smothering blanket.

Small-town life seems so encrusted with custom and so defensive in the face of change that any person might despair of accomplishing anything significantly different from accepted patterns of living. Yet we also must deal with the fact that tremendous changes have taken place in our adult lifetime. These changes have involved masses of people, but each person was first an individual who had to make a personal analysis of his or her will and a commitment to a goal.

I believe that God has answered this question for those of us who will be sensitive to what God has done in the world. James Francis has focused that answer in a piece titled "One Solitary Life":

> Here is a man who was born in an obscure village, the child of a peasant woman. He grew up in an obscure village. He worked in a carpenter shop until he was thirty, and then for three years he was an itinerant teacher. He never wrote a book. He never had a family. He never went to college. He never travelled, except in infancy, more than two hundred miles from the place where he was born. He never did one of the things that usually accompany greatness. He had no credentials but himself. While he was still a young man, the tide of popular opinion turned against him. He was turned over to his enemies. He went through the mockery of a trial. He was nailed upon a cross between two thieves. His executioners gambled for the only piece of property he had on the earth—his seamless robe. When he was dead, he was taken down from the cross and laid in a borrowed grave through the courtesy of a friend. Nineteen wide centuries have come and gone, and today he is the centerpiece of the human race and the leader of all human progress. I am well within the mark when I say that all the armies that ever marched, all the navies that ever were built, all the parliaments that ever sat, and all the kings that ever reigned, put together, have not affected the life of man upon this earth as powerfully as has this one solitary personality.[1]

[1] Ralph L. Woods, ed., *A Third Treasury of the Familiar* (New York: Macmillan Company, 1970), p. 440. Adapted from "One Solitary Life" (Anonymous).

It is highly suggestive to me that God, in infinite concern for the world, did not appoint a committee or call a convention. God sent one life as if to say that one life can have significance even in a world of mass psychology and propaganda. This is certainly not to deny the necessity and effectiveness of group action. But it is to assert that group action begins with individual initiative and commitment.

Perhaps you are thinking that my illustrations are not relevant to your situation. Lincoln is removed from us by more than merely the span of time. Jesus is unique in our consciousness. We tend to discount his prediction that we who follow him would do greater things than he did. Nevertheless, we can grasp the fact that Jesus had a great and consuming conviction.

High personal goals may contribute to more anxiety or to more of a sense of futility. It will have to suffice to assert that we must set our goals high if we expect to accomplish anything of significance.

Suppose a person *could* attach himself or herself to a significant goal for his or her life. Suppose that we could make definite progress toward the accomplishment of our goals. In the long run, what ultimate difference would it make? That is the most futile question of all. It is really a composite of the first two. The skull grinning atop the stack of books in the window still mocks our efforts. We *are* quite temporarily on this earth. This awareness can serve either as a spur to accomplishment or as a brake to initiative. We have a choice to make concerning our temporariness on the earth and the nonlasting quality of our achievements.

The realm of nature gives a good lesson in this respect. The coral atolls of the South Pacific are islands built up of the dead bodies of tiny sea creatures. Silt collects on the rocky crags. Finally life develops there. In the realm of human history we, like those coral atolls, build upon the remains of previous generations. We cannot simply say that the spiritual and cultural and scientific achievements of the past were to no purpose or significant effect. We build a moral quality into the fiber of history by the degree of our responsibility and the caliber of our morality. We contribute to the fountains that flow into the future. Those fountains will flow bitter or sweet according to our fidelity to those values that have been passed along to us in our Christian heritage.

When we are tempted to become cynical about the lasting character of personal contributions to society, we need to stop and consider whether human life would have survived this long in a world in which there were no restraints upon a person's inhumanity to another. Life is not merely a "tale told by an idiot." It becomes an opportunity for us to contribute creatively to the flow of history. The fact is that the choices we make, make *all* the difference in the life we lead: what sort of vocation, what sort of companion, what sort of destiny we choose for ourselves, what values challenge our vision, what principles sustain us. We have a choice to make and a road to travel every day. As Nietzsche said: "He who has a *why* to live can endure almost any *how*." Never, never, never give up!